THE LINGERING *Shadow*

The Lingering *Shadow*

A Story of God's Healing Power Moved Into Purpose

Linda H. Plick, D.Min.

Charleston, SC
www.PalmettoPublishing.com

Second Edition

Hardcover (dj): 979-8-8229-4218-9
Paperback: 979-8-8229-4219-6
eBook: 979-8-8229-4220-2
Audiobook: 979-8-8229-4221-9

Dedication

I dedicate this book to my mother, Ada Mae Hall, who passed away on October 21, 2011. It was her love and trust in the Lord I observed that became a powerful force in my life. As I began to write and reflect on the goodness of the Lord, I did not realize how God was always there rescuing, delivering, and keeping me during some very difficult seasons in my life.

I would like to thank Apostle Chris Esteves, Ph.D., Pastor of Lifeway Church Ministries in Rancho Cucamonga, CA, who through his weekly teachings on purpose, destiny, kings, and priests, reawakened and stirred up my vision which had become dormant. Special thanks to J. Kim Troy Curry from Inside Out Support & Services for offering her professional encouragement and coaching in bringing this book to fruition. I am also grateful for the support of all who stood with me as the late Dr. Doris G Morgan, Ph.D., trained us to overcome the adversities of life.

I would also like to express my gratitude to Barbara Emery from Lifeway Church Ministries. She played an integral role in proofreading the manuscript. Additionally, she helped me to secure a publisher, leading to the successful launch of this book.

To my sons, Reginald Shelton, Keith Thompson and daughter, Monica Shelton-Frierson, my new blended family, and my precious grand and great grandchildren. My heart's desire has been to complete

God's purpose of leaving the legacy of writing a book showing that it is never too late to pursue purpose.

I want to also thank my spiritual daughter, Yolanda Gaines, who has been there for years encouraging me to write.

Finally, and foremost, I want to dedicate this book to my husband, George R. Plick, Sr., who God brought into my life while the world was experiencing a global health crisis. As leader of the Grief and Recovery Group, he helped the members address a lifetime of losses and provided tools and skills and a path to move forward. This book is a gift I'm leaving for my family as my legacy of faith, my life story, and as a survivor of childhood trauma.

All these beautiful women have since passed on but worth mentioning as they were influential in making me the woman of God that I am today. They are as follow: Mrs. Cooper, Miss Siegel, Irma Dee Hawkins, Lola Beatrice Hall, Ethel Mae Johnson, Dr. Etta Jean Johnson, Betty Johnson, Pauline "Mama" Hardy, Isola "Dear" Pier Savant and Edith Shelton.

The Spirit of the Lord is upon Me; Because He hath anointed Me
To preach the gospel to the poor;
He has sent Me to heal the brokenhearted,
To proclaim liberty to the captives
And recovery of sight to the blind,
To set at liberty those who are oppressed;
Luke 4:18 (NKJV)

Contents

Foreword

For at least two decades, I have followed Dr. Linda Plick educating herself in biblical counseling and many subjects such as trauma, grief and loss, drug abuse, alcoholism, and mental health issues.

Dr. Linda has encouraged me as she worked at the Dr. Betty R. Price Counseling Center as a Professional Faith-Based Biblical Counselor as well as with the South Bay Behavioral Health Outpatient Center in Torrance, California. She also volunteered and ministered to incarcerated youth at the Challenger Memorial Youth Prison Center in Lancaster, CA.

She also has established and taught a Good-News After School Bible club to many children in the public school system for years. I have watched Dr. Linda Plick on her early journey in life where she ran from unresolved issues and battles. Today, she is a warrior and an overcomer. Her book will empower and impact anyone and give them a life changing view using biblical strategies. Clarity will help you understand the root of fear and how to stand against it by using the Word of God to give you the victories in Christ.

By Chaplain Emertha Jones, an Ordained Minister who served as a Counselor and Chaplain in the Los Angeles County Probation Department/Juvenile Hall, also Ministry of Chaplain's Eagles for 10 years.

Introduction

The purpose of this book is to share how childhood traumatic experiences caused me to develop a defense mechanism to protect my heart emotionally, which led to dysfunctional patterns of thinking and behaving. These traumatic events created negative impacts on my beliefs, values, and the principles I lived by, as well as my outlook on the world. As I recount them, my perspective on life was that it was unfair. I often wondered what my life would have been like if I had a choice about the family into which I was born. I did not get to pick my parents or siblings. I had no control over the timing in which I was born. I loved my family dearly and like many families, they can be dysfunctional. I was different and my perspective on life was different, so I often felt like I didn't fit. However, those were the cards I was dealt, so I learned to play my hand.

Overall, this book will explore how childhood traumas can impact a person's life and offer insights into patterns of thinking and behaving. Also, it will highlight the power of neuroplasticity, which allows the brain to change and develop new memories, skills, and abilities as it transforms a resistant negative mindset into a positive one. I am not playing the victim or blaming others, instead I am telling the story of how I overcame difficult circumstances and emerged as a strong and capable adult. Despite growing up in a dysfunctional environment, I learned early to stand tall and use each adversity as an opportunity for growth. I developed great independence and resiliency and learned to rely on no one or anything except God. However, I now understand how the traumatic experiences I endured had a deep impact on my thoughts, actions, and identity.

I've had many conversations with the Lord about my life, its meaning and purpose as I searched for answers. Why was I born? What were the purposes of all the woes? What do I value most about my life? How can I incorporate the lessons learned into my daily life? I learned to journal through each encounter for the sake of sanity and asked the Lord how to share my story as I gained insight and purpose. When I reflect over my life, my parents and family, I conclude that life happened, and it affected each of us differently. I learned that erroneous and maladaptive thinking and behavioral patterns could change. Today, I stand whole and healed and I received a release from the Lord to write my story.

I am reminded of a poem I read along this journey that spoke to my heart about God's purpose. This is where I will begin my story.

God's Purpose

I did not break you, child of mine without a purpose grand.
I did not crush you like the rose To be trodden in the sand.
I did not scatter you like the wind those pieces which I broke.
Instead, I gently picked them up such tender care I took.
I chose to make a vessel rare the kind not often found
made from those broken pieces picked up off the ground.
I broke you, precious child of mine for self can have no part.
I crushed you like the fragrant rose
that I might have your heart.
I gathered up those scattered pieces to make a vessel true.
For I desired that men should see what only God could do.
~Anonymous~

For I know the thoughts that I think toward you, saith the LORD, thoughts of peace, and not of evil, to give you an expected end.
Jeremiah 29:11 (KJV)

Purpose

Childhood trauma can have a lasting effect on one's physical and mental health, as the brain may repress memories as a coping mechanism. Trauma is not simply a scientific label for our emotions, but rather a pervasive aspect of people's everyday experiences. The effects may result in distorted thinking patterns triggered by traumatic memories, which can persist despite being accepted as tolerable. As someone who has endured trauma, when I become fearful, certain areas of my brain become more active and as a result, my cognitive abilities decrease. I move into a fight-or-flight mode, which results in reduced cognitive functioning.

In this book, my aim is not to just share how the traumatic events that occurred in my childhood had a physical and mental impact on my perspective of life, but to show how the fear and trauma associated with these events promoted unhealthy emotional responses that became my mindset well into my adulthood.

Neuroplasticity is the science that permits the brain to continue to grow and evolve in response to life experiences. Historically, research scientists believed that the brain stopped growing after childhood. However, current research has shown that the brain is able to continue growing and changing throughout one's lifespan because it can redefine negative experiences and shift the function to different regions of the brain. This shift makes it possible to change the fear associated with trauma that causes dysfunctional patterns of thinking and behaving since exposure to trauma is a change in the response of life (Psychology Today, 2023).

I experienced traumatic events as a child, which resulted in a mindset that had long-lasting physical and mental health challenges well into my adult years. This was a result of the brain repressing memories as a coping mechanism. Throughout adulthood, I always felt that something was not quite right, but I did not know why. My brain had repressed many unpleasant memories, but when I experienced fear or stress, my brain remembered and would trigger the fight-or-flight response, protecting me from losing it. My emotions ruled me, which would worsen during those stressful times. There continues to be a debate about the validity of memory repression, and it continues to be controversial in today's scientific community (Jones, 2021). With that said, I will begin my life story and the subsequent events that led to the negative and unhealthy responses in my life.

CHAPTER 1

The Knock

I encountered my first traumatic experience at the tender age of four. I was the second child born to William Shakespeare Hall and Ada Mae Hardy, both from Louisiana; Daddy from Alexandria and Mother from Shreveport. After completing high school, my father sought a better life and joined the United States Armed Services. Not long afterward, he was stationed in Bakersfield, California, where he served four years and attained the rank of Staff Sargent. During this time, the U.S. Army did not provide resources offering support to help families adapt to military life, especially for those unfamiliar with the experience. When he was honorably discharged, they had four children: Carl, me (affectionately called Kaye), William Shakespeare Jr., and Kenny. My younger sister, Katherine, was born five years later. As he transitioned to civilian life, my father faced the challenge of providing for his family. Additionally, my mother found it difficult to adjust to life in California, having never been away from home before.

As I reflect on that time, it becomes clear that more than likely, my mother's tears were caused by the overwhelming thoughts of not only adjusting to life away from her family in Louisiana, but also having her fourth child in four years. It should have been a joyful time for her, but she was experiencing postpartum blues, also known as the "baby blues." The hormonal changes in her body had caused many symptoms, including sadness, anxiety, depression, difficulty sleeping, excessive crying and maybe even thoughts of harming the baby. Yes, I believe she was overwhelmed and that's why she cried so often.

Research today indicates that postpartum blues are normal and will eventually go away as the hormones level out. It is also possible that the symptoms could continue for months or even years. Eighty-five percent of women giving birth can experience these common symptoms (Osborne, 2023). During the 1940's, the attitude was very different. If a woman had postpartum blues, it was not uncommon to be committed to an insane asylum until she conformed (Moore, 2021). Because my family did not understand what was happening to my mom, they reached out for assistance not knowing that it would be the day my family would be ripped apart.

There was a knock at the door, and two men dressed in white came and put my mother in what I later learned was a "straitjacket." They constrained her to a stretcher and put her in the van as she screamed, "Don't worry, I'm going to heaven." Traumatized with fear and panic, I simply did not understand and there was no explanation provided. So, at 4-years-old, I believed that they took my mother to heaven.

This traumatic event was the beginning of cognitive distortions and maladaptive thinking patterns that became my belief, which I buried deep in the recesses of my mind and never questioned it. Childhood trauma can have a long-lasting and pervasive effect on a person's physical, emotional, and mental health, such as anxiety, depression, and post-traumatic stress disorder (PTSD) in adulthood (Lewis, et al., 2020). Research has also shown that it is important to address or prevent adverse childhood experiences because of the long-lasting negative effects they may have. The negative experiences can shape a child's development. It can lead to issues such as poor self-esteem, lack of trust in others, and difficulties forming healthy relationships in adulthood. Therefore, it is important to work toward prevention (CDC, 2019).

CHAPTER 2

The House

After this traumatic event, our family moved from one house to the next because Dad was unable to provide for four small children: mentally, emotionally, or financially. The four of us became part of the "system" until one day Daddy came and took us to live with him in what looked like a "house church." The kind and compassionate lady of the house was named Mrs. Cooper and she loved Jesus. She welcomed us, fed us, bathed us, and put us in new pajamas.

Many would come to this house for food and prayer. She held church services and prayer meetings throughout the week in this house. In front of the fireplace was a small altar, where people would kneel and pray. As I lay in my dad's arms that night, I had only one prayer…"Thank you, God, for keeping us together and making us safe again." This house was located on 21st and Central Avenue in Los Angeles. It was warmer than all the other houses we'd lived in.

I remembered loving to slip out of bed late at night to sit on the stairs, watching Mrs. Cooper preach about Jesus and His healing power. Many people would gather to experience deliverance. They danced, played tambourines, and prayed in a babbling tongue until they passed out. As I said, Mrs. Cooper loved her some Jesus and she loved us. So, I thank God for this beautiful woman, who showed love by opening her home to my dad and his four children. She comforted many people that fell on hard times and needed a new start. The "house church" was our home for the next three years.

One day, my dad, Mrs. Cooper, and I went to visit my mom at Camarillo State Hospital. It felt like "heaven" as people were strolling around dressed in white, while we waited in a beautiful blooming garden. Eventually, a lady brought my mom out to visit us, and I was thrilled to see her again. She had been in this treatment facility for nine months. Not long after that visit, it was decided that mom was emotionally stable enough to go home and be a fulltime mother and homemaker. As a result, we eventually moved out of the "house church" and into the William Meade Housing Project. I believed that Mrs. Cooper played a significant role in bringing our family back together and by helping to bring our mom home.

I became incredibly resilient and independent, while also remaining emotionally sensitive. The experiences helped shape my perception of life, my thoughts, and my behaviors, and stayed with me throughout my formative years and beyond. Exploring the connections between these events and the lingering shadow has been an ongoing journey for me.

CHAPTER 3
The Click

Prior to the introduction of automatic washing machines in the late 30's, people used manual methods to clean their clothes. They rubbed them, pounded them, boiled them, and washed them. We had the old wringer washer, and my job was to help by putting the washed clothes through the wringer.

I remember this day so well because as I performed this task, somehow, my arm got entrenched with the clothes, and I was traumatized because my arm went right in along with the clothes. I pulled but could not stop the flow. Fear and panic gripped me. There was no one around to help me, so I thought I was going to go through the wringer with the clothes. Then, there was this miraculous "click," and the wringer stopped. Through a miracle, God rescued me and saved my arm. I don't think I ever shared this event with anyone. I just buried the thought. To this day, the memory still traumatizes me, but I find peace and comfort when I imagine myself wrapped in the loving arms of Jesus.

For years, I harbored that experience without realizing that fear was rooted and connected to the event. Whenever triggered, I experienced an overwhelming sensation, akin to a massive monster consuming me and no one came to help. Bringing tears to my eyes, my response and coping mechanism has been to run—and run I did. I lived life in a fight-or-flight response to the difficulties I encountered. Again, I used imagery as my coping strategy, and it worked for me whenever I needed to experience peace and comfort. Still, I never realized the connection to the trauma I experienced in my childhood and my responses, which controlled my life whenever I encountered trying situations as an adult.

Back in the day, kids loved to play the game, Hide and-Seek. My brothers and I did too. Every time I hid, they would find me. So, one day I saw that old icebox sitting in the corner of the yard and thought, "If I hide there, for sure they wouldn't find me." It had to be the perfect hiding spot, so I crawled in, and the door accidentally locked behind me and I couldn't escape. I screamed and bang on the door hoping it would open. I could hear them, but they couldn't hear me. It was dark. I felt cramped. I felt trapped. I couldn't move and felt totally helpless. I became exhausted and was about to pass out when I heard that miraculous "click." The door unlocked, I saw light and fell out. Everyone was gone. God had miraculously saved me from destruction again.

In the late 1930's, iceboxes were replaced with electric refrigerators for those that lived during the era of our grandparents. Some of us may remember the iceboxes. Lower income families continued to use their iceboxes well into the 1940's. Back in the day, many young children, while playing hide-and-seek, would crawl into them and suffocate. In North Carolina, a child died. As a result, in 1955, the state passed a law making it a misdemeanor for a person to abandon, discard, or store a refrigerator—or an icebox or similar apparatus – without first detaching its doors, hinges, latches and lids, to ensure a child couldn't become trapped (American Legal, 2022). I was trapped but the Lord had another plan for my life.

For years, the weight of a lingering shadow stayed with me, and I suffered from agoraphobia, which according to the DSM-5-TR (APA, 2022) is marked with fear, anxiety, or stress when in an enclosed place. The fear was all-consuming. That onetime experience may have generated symptoms of post-traumatic stress disorder (PTSD), which may have occurred within one month of the event or possibly years afterward. For me, it took years, or at least I never connected fear and anxiety to adverse childhood experiences when I encountered stressful situations throughout my life. I was a survivor and had developed a fight-or-flight response as my coping mechanism. It wasn't normal, but it was appropriate for survival at the time as it allowed me to continue necessary activities, regulate emotions, and to keep my self-esteem intact (SAMHSA, 2014).

CHAPTER 4

The Cross

Another extraordinary experience is that while living in the William Meade Housing Project aka "Dogtown," I met a small, framed lady with hair white as snow. She stood a little taller than I did. She found me playing under a tree near the railroad tracks and introduced herself as Miss Siegel.

My mother always told me to not to talk with strangers, but I felt a sense of knowing that this time it was okay. She carried a shopping bag of goodies and told me she had a friend she wanted to share with me. I became very curious. She began to pull out all kinds of pictures, cards, games, and a tiny book. The tiny white book was the New Testament and she told me that Jesus loved me and wanted me to have it. She also told me to read it whenever I felt sad, lonely, or disappointed.

Miss Siegel became my friend and each day I would meet her at the tree as she shared stories about her friend. After a few days, Miss Siegel told me that there was a part of the story she wanted me to see but she needed me to take her to my home to meet my mother and get permission to go see the ending of the story. When my mother met Miss Siegel, she invited her in, and agreed to let me go with her.

Miss Siegel and I caught the old red streetcar that ran down the tracks on North Main Street and later we caught a bus. We arrived at this huge park and went past an iron gate. We saw beautiful flowers all along the hillside. The crowd was enormous, and we had to wait in a long line to get into the theater. It was a dramatic, narrated presentation with music of the crucifixion of Jesus. We were at Forest Lawn Cemetery in Glendale. Once inside, they handed us specialty glasses to wear, designed to give a three-dimensional view, which enhanced our depth perception, placing us into the crowd depicted on the giant movie screen.

We stood at the foot of the cross. In the background were three crosses, two were erected and one was on the ground being prepared to be raised. The narration was so loud and vivid as the story of the crucifixion of Jesus played out. The angry and hateful crowd mocked Jesus. He was to be nailed to the cross along with the two thieves. John, one of His beloved disciples, was there as well as Simon of Cyrene, the man who helped carry Jesus' cross up the mountain. Mary, the mother of Jesus, Martha, and Mary Magdalene were in the distance, grief stricken and praying for a miracle. The angry crowd was there to carry out the persecution. There were two men, one on Jesus' right and one on the left. Jesus stood there to be nailed and hung on the cross in the middle. There lying beside Him was a red robe and a crown of thrones, to be placed on His head. He endured the cross never saying a mumbling word.

The purpose of this presentation was to deliver a message of love, forgiveness, and salvation to all men, women, boys, and girls, to believe in the Lord Jesus Christ and accept His work on the cross. It was that message, that presentation, that story of Jesus hanging on the cross that burned forever in my heart. He was not guilty of any crime but endured shame and horror as He hung there in disgrace before the crowd that wanted nothing but His death. It appeared that they had won, but He conquered death. I cried and cried, and at that time, I declared that I would never act in a way that would cause pain or grief in His heart.

That day, I received Him into my heart and decided that He would be my friend forever. Miss Siegel and I caught the bus and then the old red streetcar back home. I remember feeling so broken and hurt that Jesus had died. I was silent but Miss Siegel had a gentle way of making me understand, connecting the event we had just witnessed as God's greatest demonstration of love to all mankind. The only response was to believe and receive Jesus Christ into one's heart and His gift of eternal life. I did.

The next day, I was so excited and went to the tree and subsequent days later, but never saw Miss Siegel again. I was sad and disappointed but then I remembered she had given me that tiny, white New Testament to read when I needed comforting. That was in 1951. I was seven years old.

As an adult, I have returned to Forest Lawn Cemetery in Glendale and the Crucifixion-Resurrection display and unbelievably, that masterpiece is still there! A Polish painter named Jan Styka shared a dream about Christ's execution with his close friend, Ignace Paderewski. Styka was so inspired that he ultimately created an impressive painting, detailing the event of the execution and others. He began the work in 1894. It took him six years to finish, and it is the largest religious painting in the world. Before he completed it, he travelled to Jerusalem to ask for Pope Leo XIII's blessing on his palette. It measured 195' in length and 45' in height, the width of a four-lane highway. He managed to show it once in 1902 in Russia.

The painting eventually was loaded onto a boat and brought to America in hopes of finding a place for it. It was so large that it had to be stored in a warehouse in New York. There was a fire, and Styka's other paintings were destroyed but miraculously, this painting was saved. Because it was so large, Styka tried to raise money to pay the custom fees but had to return to his country without it. As a result, the American government seized it, and it was lost for 40 years. In 1944, Mr. Hubert Eaton, the founder of Forest Lawn Cemetery, heard about its existence, and was intrigued by the story and began a search to recover it. Eventually, it was in the basement of the Chicago Civic Opera Company. Mr. Eaton purchased it and had a permanent display built in the Hall of the Crucifixion at the Forest Lawn Cemetery in Glendale, California (Anda, 2022).

I, too, was intrigued because I had seen the display in 1951. So, in 2019, I went back to the Forest Lawn Cemetery to see if it was a dream or was it real. Wow! It was real! It is a must see. However, there was no crowd. I saw a mother or two sitting there with their children viewing the painting. It was quiet and lifeless, no noise, no special glasses to wear but it still touched my heart because I'll never forget what Jesus experienced for me and all of mankind. I rededicated my life and renewed my commitment to Jesus. I thought, 'Where is the crowd? Where are the people?'

In 2019, the COVID-19 virus caused a global pandemic. The world shut down. I was an essential worker, continuing to work and was given a pass by my employer to travel the freeways. I continued to attend church during that season but found that people were fearful of catching this deadly virus and they eventually stopped going anywhere, especially to church. I continued to go but the crowd got smaller and smaller until the government finally shut the churches down and eventually, everything went virtual. I was fearful of what was happening to America. Are we losing our freedom to go to church and worship the Lord? I was petrified and later learned that this pandemic had gone global.

Fear and panic became my struggle because the "church" was my sustaining force in life. It was my sanctuary. What was happening to America? I just couldn't tolerate the thought of not being able to worship freely. I reflected and remembered Miss Siegel, who had a saying that she demonstrated with her hands, "This is the church, this is the steeple, look inside, and see all the people." However, when I do that little gesture with my hands today, I say, "This is the church, this is the steeple, look inside, and ***where are the people?***" Thank God for TV and the internet, as I was able to attend various churches all over the world via YouTube. My coping strategy during COVID-19 was to pray, praise and spend time with God, the sustaining force that brought me through. The church is now open again, but it breaks my heart to see the world becoming more and more indifferent towards the things of God.

Be strong and be courageous. Do not fear or be in dread of them
for it is the Lord our God who goes with you.
He will never leave you or forsake you.
Deuteronomy 31:6 (ESV)

CHAPTER 5

The Fall

My amazing mother played a significant role in the shaping of whom I am today. She passed down her resilience and steadfast faith of being fixed and unmovable to her children. We attended Metropolitan Baptist Church on Hooper Avenue, a place of my fondest memories. Our lives were enriched with memories of singing in the junior choir, ushering, attending BYTU on Sunday evening and Vacation Bible School in the summer. Miss Siegel's wise words resonated with me, "You can continue to learn about our friend when you go to church." Those words stayed with me, and I thank God that my mother made it a habit of attending church frequently: Sunday mornings, Sunday nights, Wednesday nights, and even programs on Saturdays were our way of life. Thanks to my mother, our church community and even Miss Siegel because the seeds they planted in my heart has grounded me in the love of Jesus.

My mom loved to talk to the Lord and He would give her dreams and visions. Whenever she would experience one, I would tune in intently, for I believed she heard from God. I remember a dream that she shared continuously because it was troubling, and she was trying to make sense of it. She talked about a lady sitting in a corner of a room crying. People would come by, and she would tell them this troubling dream and they would try to comfort her but couldn't. Days would pass and she would still say, "I wonder what that dream meant." Weeks passed. Then one day, she received a phone call. It was the hospital saying that my dad had an accident and that she should come to the hospital immediately. I was about 15 years of age, so we caught the bus and went to the hospital.

I have come to understand that dreams and visions can be a powerful message from God and sometimes, they can even provide a warning. I believe my mother's dream was a premonition of what was to come, even though she didn't fully understand its meaning at that time. This was another distressing incident, which had a devastating effect on our family. My dad did not recover from the tragic fall. He was a painter, and the scaffolding on which he stood had broken and he fell to his death. My mother now was a single parent responsible for rearing five children; Katherine, the youngest was seven and Carl, the oldest, was sixteen. We had to cope with life without our dad and it was just not fair. I have learned to cope by cherishing the memories of my father, holding on to them knowing that one day we will all reunite in heaven.

Kenny, my youngest brother, was about eleven, and was with Dad when he fell. In reflection, he witnessed that horrible accident and the potential impact it would have on him went unnoticed by everyone. By the time he became an adolescent, the warning signs were there but no one knew what to do. He began to display behavioral problems and later diagnosed as schizophrenic, beginning a lifetime journey of mental health issues.

Seventy years ago, people were silent and lacked an understanding of how to deal with a loved one who exhibited symptoms of my brother's mental health condition. No one knew then about the National Alliance on Mental Illness (NAMI), whose role was to end the silence. Today it has become the nation's largest evidence based grassroots mental health organization, dedicated to building better lives for the millions of Americans affected by mental illness. Through dialogue, their goal is to grow the movement, to end the stigma, to effectively give knowledge, and change attitudes toward mental health conditions (NAMI, 2002). Kenny is my hero and has had a life of rejection because people did not know how to treat him. He is strong and resilient and is a real trooper with a heart of gold. He is now seventy-five and living in an assisted living facility. I pray that God will continue to keep an open door until He takes him home.

My sister, Katherine, continues to advocate for Kenny, who is a participant of the continuum of mental health services, funded and shared by Medicaid and private insurance to address the unique needs of this diverse population. Other funding sources include the Indian Health Services, Tricare, NAMI, and United Way, self-pay and private grants for mental health intervention services, mental health assessment and partial hospitalization. Individuals experiencing a mental health crisis are connected for appropriate mental health treatment through a peer-operated hotline and warmlines, which include licensed and/or credentialed clinicians there to assess them within the mental health crisis services system. NAMI continues to provide training to a unit that specializes in responding to people with mental illness, support residential programs and provide substance abuse and mental health services (SAMHSA 2020).

CHAPTER 6

The Race

I developed resilience by facing and adapting to various situations and challenges in life. To cope, I would often resort to the fight-or-flight response. One day, while warming up for my gym class, I discovered my aptitude for running through the Girls' Athletic Club. I decided to join the first Women's AAU Track and Field club that met at my school. My passion for running continued to grow and eventually I became a skilled athlete, clocking an impressive 6 flat in the 50-yard dash and 11.6 seconds in the 100-yard relay. That earned me a spot as the anchor relay person in the 440-relay at the 1962 Invitational Track and Field Competition at the Sports Arena in Los Angeles. It was an incredible experience as I was able to compete with the Olympic star Wilma Rudolph who, despite her challenges, had become a highly successful track and field athlete, having already won three gold medals at the 1960 Olympic Games.

Wilma Rudolph's determination and perseverance served as my inspiration to succeed, for I also wanted to make it to the Olympics. When I ran, it soothed so much of the emotional pain I carried. I grew up during a time when the neighborhood I lived in experienced hunger, poverty, sickness, diseases, gangs, juvenile delinquency, graffiti, teen pregnancies, drugs, and alcohol abuse. Additionally, there were the gamblers, who would shoot "craps" as they stood around the liquor stores, which seemed to be on every corner. I had those taunting memories of my dad rolling dice with the fellows when I was very young, living on 21st and Central. I find it amusing how my mother would instinctively know when my father had won enough money and she would go down to the corner where he was, scoop up his earnings, and then go to the grocery store to purchase the necessities for our family. She would preach to those men attempting to discourage them from continuing to indulge in their sinful habits of drinking and gambling.

Yes, it was memories like those that fueled my motivation and my dedication to continue to run. Running in the Invitationals qualified me to compete in the Nationals held in Corpus Christi, Texas. Unfortunately, my dreams of making it to the 1964 Olympics in Rome were crushed when my mother vetoed the idea. She didn't believe sports were for girls, but rather their place was in the home, washing, ironing, cooking, and cleaning and not running races. "Leave that to the boys," she would say and that's how that conversation ended. I was crushed and buried that huge disappointment. "Life was just not fair" was my response. As a result, I adapted a new attitude to soothe the pain and disappointments. I learned to "take the licking and keep on ticking."

Despite this major setback, I continued to find solace and peace through my fight-or-flight response to stress. America was experiencing tumultuous times. I guess that's why I grew to love the movie, *Forrest Gump* with Tom Hanks. Hanks' character journaled about the significant events of the 60's and 70's. The themes and morals of America were daunting. America was experiencing trauma and life was unpredictable. There was the Vietnam War, the assassinations of two men, President J. F. Kennedy and his brother, Robert Kennedy. The Civil Rights Movement brought demonstrations and riots and finally, the assassination of another great leader, Dr. Martin Luther King, Jr. As if this was not enough, the economy was struggling with dropping stock prices, long gas lines, and skyrocketing inflation at over 12 percent.

The Watergate scandal involving President Nixon also brought social wounds that ran deep. To promote healing and unity in our country, Richard Milhous Nixon, our 38th President, resigned on August 9, 1974, leaving the office to the charge of Gerald R. Ford, his Vice President. I still have that L. A. Times newspaper article with the headlines, "Nixon Quit!" L. A. Times, (1974). Despite the adversities and traumatic events that impacted us all, America persevered.

Forrest Gump also experienced trauma due to the tone of the environment. I guess one day he needed to express himself, so while waiting for the bus, he began to share his perspective of these turbulent events with a woman he didn't even know. In his young life, he too had experienced trauma. He was born with polio and had to wear braces. To add to this, he was often bullied by his classmates, causing him to run. One day, while dealing with their taunting, he heard that inner voice says, "Run, Forrest, run!" He ran so hard that he shed the braces on his legs. This was a turning point in his life, and he was never the same. His story made a great impact on me and the world (Zemeckis, 1994). Wow! So incredible. So, like Forrest Gump, I ran and ran and ran. One day, he stopped. Just like that. He looked around but hadn't realize that he had influenced a whole crowd of people to run right behind him. I guess many people have learned to "run" in response to the stresses of life.

The Bible speaks about endurances and facing hardships. 2 Timothy 2:3 (NIV) states, *"Join with me in suffering, like a good soldier of Jesus Christ."* 2 Timothy 4:7 (NIV) says, *"I have fought the good fight, I have finished the race, I have kept the faith."* These verses encourage me to stay strong in the face of adversity. As athletes train, they learn that there will be pain and suffering as they prepare for a significant race. The purpose of training is to teach us to endure the pain and difficulties to achieve goals, dreams, and purposes. Today, I continue to rely on God's strength and His Word to overcome any challenges that may come my way and most importantly, to remain steadfast in my faith. The ultimate lessons I've learned about my life have been to not focus on the "*whys*" but to *continue* to cultivate godliness, faith and patience in all areas of life and to allow the Holy Spirit to teach and guide me when making decisions. I've also learned to trust God especially when you don't understand the purpose of the adversities.

5) *Trust in the Lord with all your heart,*
And lean not on your own understanding;
6) *In all your ways acknowledge Him,*
And He shall direct your paths.
Proverbs 3:5,6 (NKJV)

CHAPTER 7

The Earthquake

One day, in 1994, there was the Northridge earthquake. It occurred about 4:30 AM. I lived in Palmdale and commuted to my job in the Los Angeles Civic Center. We had to leave about 5:00 AM to be on the 14 Freeway in time to avoid heavy traffic and we had not yet gotten the word about the damages caused by the earthquake. The interchange connectors on Highway 14 and Highway 5 had collapsed. As we approached that area, the freeway came to a complete halt. It was dark and I was driving the 12-passenger van. I felt trapped. Fear and panic consumed me. It was like the fear I experienced when locked in that icebox. I was overwhelmed and had vaguely dealt with the symptoms, which had become this lingering shadow that would trigger a negative response whenever I found myself in a tight space.

Today was one of those days. I couldn't run as I was accustomed to doing. I felt trapped and overwhelmed. I couldn't breathe and thought I was going to die. I was having a panic attack and began to quietly pray and cry out to the Lord to keep me from losing my mind. It was this experience of feeling trapped on that freeway, in the van, in the dark, that sent me straight to therapy to deal with the root of this fear and anxiety.

While writing this book, I continued to ask the Lord why it is necessary to share all these negative experiences I call "woes." He revealed that my core beliefs, cognitive distortions, behaviors and attitudes about the world and myself, were deeply rooted in my childhood experiences, which required a shift. For Him to change those negative mindsets, He must begin with my inner self, my heart. Proverbs 4:8 reminds me that wisdom and insight are crucial for growth. Proverbs 23:7 (NKJV) says, *"For as he thinks in his heart, so is he. "Eat and drink!" he says to you, but his heart is not with you."* Imagine, being saved but your heart is not with the Lord.

One of the most amazing gifts that God has given us is the human mind. We can learn, to think, to choose and to reason. Our thoughts become a reflection of who we really are. We can say one thing with our mouth, but our hearts can be in a completely different place and so often, we do that. The inclinations of our heart shapes the reality of who we are, and our thoughts shape our behavior.

A lot of childhood trauma affected my life and finally, it was important for me to confront my past wounds with courage and humility, so I could be healed and whole. I have had to trust God completely on this journey of seeking His strength and guidance, as I revisited those dark places and dealt with that lingering shadow. My hope is to continue to gain wisdom and insight as I continue to heal and thrive confronting one layer of fear at a time.

"Wisdom is the principal thing: Therefore, get wisdom.
And in all your getting, get understanding."
Proverbs 4:7 (NKJV)

CHAPTER 8
The Helper

The Missing Ingredient the Gift of the Holy Spirit

As I grew older, I continued to press toward the higher calling and I've rededicated my life and commitment in my heart to the Lord, my Savior, and my Friend. I found that it is essential to begin each day praying and meditating on the Word of God. I've had to allow this love to seep deep within the recesses of my inner being. Seemingly, I had closed off my heart and the truth is that God's presence was not with me. In fact, in one therapy session, the psychologist concluded by telling me he had gone as far as he could go because I wore an "apron around my heart" to protect it and only God could penetrate it and bring healing. So even though I would praise Him before entering His presence, I did so presenting this pretentious, "cleaned up" self to the Lord. I experienced much trauma and had many wounds, but my truth was that I was shut away from the Light, allowing those deep inner wounds to fester. I did not think of them as sins, but rather, unresolved issues that I'd stuffed deep within. They were buried deep (Young, 2014). Therefore, even though saved and transformed, when I came to the Lord I deceived myself "thinking" I had been transformed.

Don't get me wrong, I'm sure that I went through a miraculous change. I felt "brand new." The "old person" did indeed die and behold I did become this "new person." The more I studied the Word of God, the more I grew and one day, I stumbled and fell and that "old person" I thought had died, came to the surface. I felt like Apostle Paul when he said in Romans 7:15-20, *"I don't really understand myself, for I want to do what is right, but I don't do it. Instead, I do what I hate. But if I know that what I am doing is wrong, this shows that I agree that the law is good. So, I am not the one doing wrong; it is sin living in me that does it. And I know that nothing good lives in me, that is, in my sinful nature. I want to do what is right, but I can't. I want to do what is good, but I don't. I don't want to do what is wrong, but I do it anyway. But if I do what I don't want to do, I am not really the one doing wrong it is sin living in me that does it."*

What was this lingering shadow that hovered over me, keeping me in a constant struggle to make the right decisions or to do the right thing? The memory wars were constant. Most researchers today believe that it is rare to forget trauma completely that occurred early in the childhood and that "recovered memories" are not always accurate (Otgaar, H. (2019). This explanation left me feeling perplexed, as a result, I continued my journey to find the answers.

I wanted to be better and reach my fullest potential. It was when I received the baptism of the Holy Spirit, with the evidence of speaking in tongues, that I "truly" became this "new man." That lingering shadow lifted. In Ephesians 4:22, Apostle Paul states that we need to put off the former conduct of the "old man" because he is corrupt, deceitful, and has evil desires and is hostile to the things of God. Receiving the gift of the Holy Spirit transformed my life and caused me to live in another dimension. I received a spiritual connection and gained revelation knowledge from the Holy Scriptures which empowered me to overcome any challenges or circumstances that come my way. That same transforming spiritual power comes from being born-again from God and is available today to every believer.

Who is the Holy Spirit? First, the Holy Spirit is a person just as God and His Son – not a force or influence. He possesses intellect, emotions and will. Romans 8:9, refers to the Holy Spirit as the Spirit of Christ. John 16:13, refers to Him as the Spirit of truth and Hebrew 9:14 refers to Him as the Spirit of grace. The Holy Spirit is God's agent that indwells, leads, guides, teaches, convicts one of sin and causes a new spiritual birth and transformation and empowers that believer to overcome adversities and to reflect a Christ-like nature.

CHAPTER 9

The Impact

The word "trauma" derives from the Greek word meaning, "wound." In the *Diagnostic and Statistical Manual of Mental Disorders* (DSM-IV-TR), (APA, 2000, p. 467), trauma and exposure to trauma is defined as experiencing, witnessing, or being confronted with "a traumatic event that can stem from a variety of sources, including a single incident such as a natural disaster, crime, accident, or the loss of a loved one. Interpersonal trauma involves an event in which a person has been hurt by interaction with other people. It could be a stranger, acquaintance, friend or loved one. On the other hand, it can come from recurring experiences such as abuse, violence, and neglect and can leave the individual struggling to cope and function in their daily lives. These types of traumas inflicted by others can be significantly challenging to overcome. While individual responses to trauma can vary, there are some common symptoms often reported. It is important to note that the event itself is not what causes trauma, but rather the extent to which the individual is harmed or wounded by the event.

Repeated experiences such as childhood abuse, neglect, intimate partner violence, or sexual abuse can be significantly harder to overcome. Research has reported the following are some regularly reported impacts of childhood trauma responses (Cook, et al., 2005):

- Cognition: (Impaired memory problems, inability to express oneself, making it harder for individuals to adapt to find solutions to challenges, problem-solving, negative self-beliefs, and self-evaluation).
- Brain Development: (Language delay, lower verbal IQ, smaller hippocampal, difficulty with memory tasks, significantly poorer attention, and executive function).
- Emotional challenges: (Anger, sadness, shame, anxiety, numbness, feeling overwhelmed, etc.). Hypervigilance, constantly on alert.
- Physical health issues link childhood trauma to increased risk of issues such as fatigue, nausea, muscle, tremors, and hyperarousal. Studies have linked childhood trauma with increased risk of chronic conditions like heart disease, diabetes, obesity, and autoimmune disorders. Chronic stress experienced during childhood can lead to dysregulation of the body's response system which can have long-term effects on overall health.
- Mental health issues (Depression, anxiety, negative self-image/ low self-esteem or self-worth, lack of confidence and feelings of unworthiness, posttraumatic stress disorder [PTSD], suicidality and substance abuse).
- Behavioral challenges: (Avoidant behavior, high risk behaviors, sleep and appetite disturbances, difficulties in relationship and forming and maintain healthy relationships, fear of abandonment or rejection, emotional intimacy, and challenges with boundaries and communication in both personal and professional relationships.
- Relationship difficulties: Trust issues (Attachment problems/ disorders, poor social interactions, difficulty forming relationships

with peers, intergenerational cycles of abuse and neglect, and problems in romantic relationships).

- Existential/Spiritual: (Religious trauma considered a type of betrayal trauma, where a trusted person is the source of harm. Divorce, bullying, rejection, neglect, betrayal, or abuse are all traumatic).

Trauma sets off responses in every area, be it emotional, physical, and psychological. A healthcare provider should deal with trauma that continues beyond a month, such as flashbacks, nightmares or any symptoms causing significant distress or dysfunction. According to research, there is also a link between the exposure of substance use or addiction and its effect on a trauma related disorder. Individuals that have experienced traumatic events such as child abuse, criminal attack, disaster, war, or other trauma, often turn to alcohol or drugs to help them deal with the emotional pain, the bad memories, the guilt, shame, anxiety, or error. The cycle then continues, and substance use is often a traumatic experience that produces trauma-related disorders (ISTSS, 2023).

Additionally, a deep imprint can be left on the mind as well as the body and its impact can be recognized immediately or years later (Simone, 2021). By working to recognize and identify a cognitive distortion, irrational thought patterns, emotions, or core beliefs, one can change the mindset and improve the quality of life (SAMHSA, 2023). A traumatized child can learn to wear masks that launched alienation, unhealthy defenses, and distorted cognition. Most importantly, resistance to change is evidence of that lingering shadow, which indeed can be changed from negative, maladaptive, distorted, irrational thoughts and behaviors to a healthy mindset.

with peers, intergenerational cycles of abuse and neglect, and problems in romantic relationships).

* Existential/Spiritual (Religious trauma considered a type of betrayal trauma, where a trusted person is the source of harm. Divorce, bullying, rejection, neglect, betrayal, and abuse are all traumatic)

CHAPTER 10

The Treatments

Children might experience trauma that may include childhood physical and sexual abuse, emotional abuse of persistent emotional mistreatment or neglect, humiliation, rejection or threats, surviving a natural or political disaster or being a witness to a wide range of violent events such as domestic violence, armed conflicts, gang violence, natural disasters, loss of homes, separation from family members, immigrants fleeing their countries and bullying. The psychological impact that trauma can have on children can vary widely and there can be a variety of ways that a child can react to being traumatized. Some children experience traumatic events without an apparent ill effect. Some will have long-term consequences resulting in serious psychological, physical, substance abuse, personality problems, depression, or suicide (Vitelli, 2012).

In many cases, traumatized children can develop full-blown post-traumatic stress disorder. According to the *Diagnostic and Statistical Manual of Mental Disorders* – Fifth Edition - Text Revision DSM-5-TR, the symptoms to be aware of are recurring or distressing memories, recurring dreams, or flashbacks that resemble or symbolize the traumatic event. Negative alterations in cognitions and moods associated with the traumatic events, reckless or self-destructive behavior, problems with concentration, sleep disturbance (staying awake, restless sleep), irritable behavior, (expressed as verbal or physical aggression toward people or objects) are just some of the symptoms associated with unresolved exposure to trauma. If trauma has not been resolved in children, the long-term impact can be carried into adulthood (APA, 2022).

The first step in seeking treatment to begin the healing process is to find a licensed mental health professional, who can provide a supportive environment to help one understand him or herself. There are many types of therapy helpful with the impact of childhood trauma. The goal of a mental health professional is to help identify and correct destructive thoughts and behaviors that can impact an individual over a lifetime. Traumatic events experienced during childhood are not likely forgotten but the details can be repressed, and emotional reactions can return. Therefore, the goal of the professional would be to help identify and process the emotions that may re-traumatize or overwhelm the individual. This needs to be dealt with in a safe and supportive environment as memories emerge.

IT IS IMPORTANT TO BE INFORMED. HERE ARE SOME TRAUMA FOCUSED THERAPIES FOR COMPARISON.

TYPE OF THERAPY

- Cognitive Behavioral Therapy (CBT). This treatment works well for many problems and is better than other treatments because its focus is on providing practical skills and strategies that individuals can use in their daily lives. (Chand, 2022).

Therapy Modality

- This psychotherapy is the gold standard to treat a variety of mental health conditions. CBT is rooted in the idea that most emotional and behavioral reactions come from our way of thinking about ourselves and the world around us (Gonzalez, Prendes (2012). It helps an individual to recognize negative thinking patterns and guidance to change them. Eventually, it will make you feel better and more capable in your life. (APA, 2023)

Therapy Goals & Duration Treatment Goals:

- Recognize and challenge cognitive distortions by restructuring feelings, behavioral responses, and overall emotional regulations. Focus on developing coping skills. The goal is to identify negative beliefs and transform them into more positive influences. Identifying mood and behavioral reactions have proven to be helpful for many. The most important thing is to find a qualified professional where one feels comfortable working with and opening up to.

Benefits:

- Long term results is highly effective and an effective alternative to medicine. Treatment is short. Problem-solving and time management in many aspects of life. Individual learns problem-solving skills, improves coping skills and time management.

Duration:

- Short-term. Online, In-Person. One-on-one, groups or on your own; 10-30 sessions, one session per week. (PsychCentral, 2021)

TYPE OF THERAPY

- Prolonged Exposure Therapy (PET). A specific type of cognitive behavioral therapy for posttraumatic stress disorder. It is a form of psychotherapy for unwanted thoughts, disturbing nightmares, feelings of hopelessness and depression.

Therapy Modality

- Brain learns to connect or associate with trauma. Teaches individuals to gradually re-engage with life especially things avoided. It is based on associative learning by connecting and associating. Strengthen one's ability to distinguish safety from danger. Appropriate for people who experienced a traumatic event but not necessary for those without a diagnosis.

Therapy Goals & Duration Treatment Goals:

- **Goals:** Strongly recommended for treatment of PTSD. Involves retelling traumatic experiences, exploring thoughts and feelings, to decrease unwanted traumatic reminders, using deep, slow breath to calm oneself through processing.
- **Benefits:** Helps decrease unwanted traumatic reminders and feel less distress when recalling. Learn breathing retraining to calm oneself.
- **Duration**: 60 to 120-minute sessions, 2 months or longer than 15 weeks; single or one-on-one therapy, intensive workshops, or seminars with therapists. Online, In-Person, Over phone (McLean, et al., 2011).

TYPE OF THERAPY

Systematic Desensitization or Exposure Therapy was developed by psychiatrist Joseph Wolphe.

Therapy Modality

- Create a list and rate fear hierarchy scale 1-10, work through list, use muscle relaxation techniques/classical conditioning skills to relax in the midst of fears to overcome phobia by replacing fear & anxiety in a state of calm or relaxation.

Therapy Goals & Duration Treatment Goals:

- **Goal:** To tackle fear in a safe environment using combined relaxation, mindfulness, or meditation techniques to cope and become more aware of thoughts and feelings in fearful situations.
- **Aim:** Mindfulness for the present moment to reduce anxious thoughts to overcome a phobia.
- **Duration:** Online. In Person.
  4 to 6 sessions. May need 12 (Maypole, 2019)

Type of Therapy

Eye Movement Desensitization and Reprocessing (EMDR). Developed by Dr. Rancin Shapiro in 1987 to treat post-traumatic stress disorder (PTSD).

Therapy Modality

EMDR is considered a new, nontraditional form of psychotherapy. It is used mostly to treat PTSD or trauma responses. EMDR helps the brain process and release traumatic memories in an unusual way—through our eye movements.

Therapy Goals & Duration Treatment Goals:

- **Goal:** Uses eye movements (or sometimes rhythmic tapping) to change the way a memory is stored in the brain, allowing you to "reprocess" a disturbing memory to help you move past it.

- **Aim:** To help individuals work through painful memories with your body's natural functions to recover from the effects of trauma by changing the way the traumatic memories are stored in the brain. The brain cannot tell the difference between the past and the present.
- **Duration:** 1 or 2 sessions per week totaling 6 to 12 sessions. Gillette, (2021)

SUMMARY

There are many forms of therapy that have proven to be successful, but I conceptualize Cognitive Behavioral Therapy (CBT) more effective because the foundation of CBT is dealing with thoughts that causes feelings that affects the behavior. The impact of childhood trauma affects how an individual views themselves, experiences, and their world. If thoughts about a situation are good, it causes a good emotional response. If the thought is irrational or distorted, it can cause a bad emotional response. The foundation of CBT is dealing with thoughts that affect behavior. It provides tools and strategies to manage distressing emotions, copes with triggers and helps to develop a healthier coping mechanism. An individual can work with a therapist and learn to shift from a mindset that has negative and irrational thoughts and change by identifying and challenging negative beliefs and replacing thoughts with ones that are more positive and realistic (Therapist Aide, 2022).

Childhood trauma can indeed have a long-lasting impact on an individual and if addressed, an individual can break free from the cycle of negative self-perception, self-blame, and self-destructive behavior. Life does present challenges, but a changed mindset allows the individual to view themselves, experiences, and their world healthier.

CHAPTER 11

Change Thoughts, Change Behavior

Highlights About 2023

In 2023, I came to the realization that "fight or flight" had been my survival mode for coping with life's challenges. Now that I've gained a deeper understanding of the impact of trauma, I began to stand on the power of the Scriptures to manifest my healing. So, I took a tremendous leap of faith to write this memoir. I had started engaging in fear-reducing activities and managed to suppress the "fight or flight" response to stress, which made me feel prepared to begin writing. However, when I started to revisit my childhood memories, the lingering shadow triggered the mindset of negative thinking and behaving that remained stubbornly resistant to change. I became fearful and traumatized and immediately went into that survival mode of coping. I took a brave step to gain knowledge and skills in this field. So, I enrolled in Grand Canyon University Online to get a post-master's graduate certification in this field and continued the journey of working toward healing and helping others who may have experienced similar challenges.

The course gave me an even clearer understanding of the connection between childhood trauma and its lasting impact on adults. My childhood trauma had indeed affected my life and had shaped my perspective and my behaviors throughout my life. Once I recognized its impact, I began to address the impact to promote healing and well-being. Whether the trauma was the result of a terrible one-time event or childhood experiences, I learned to use CBT to identify faulty or unhealthy ways of thinking and learn patterns of unhealthful behavior. CBT is widely recognized as an effective approach. It focuses on teaching an individual's better ways of coping by relieving symptoms and helping them be more effective in their daily lives (APA, 2023).

I came to realize that the lingering shadow did indeed have a profound impact on various aspects of my life. That lingering shadow ultimately led to a mixture of positive and negative consequences resulting from childhood trauma that I carried well into adulthood. Yes, the goal of this book has been met as I've shared my story. My journey specifically details how this dark *lingering shadow* controlled my thoughts and behaviors and prevented me from realizing and reaching my full potential as intended by God. I, literally, was controlled by my emotions because I buried one traumatic experience after another and carried them well into my adulthood that kept me running. I had no peace. I literally lived in the flight and flight mode and was ruled by distorted emotions.

Trauma affects everyone, and while some people can move forward without lasting negative effects, others may struggle for years with resolved issues or just accept that change was impossible. However, I did not lose faith and believed I could change. So, how did change happen? Well, I worked with a therapist using CBT to address and deal with many negative and unresolved issues that caused doubt and fear. I learned to identify triggers and employ coping strategies that dealt with the mind and the body that controlled behavior. I then learned to move to the spiritual realm where I discovered how to apply the Word of God to change behavior that was contrary to the lifestyle of a Believer. Finally, and foremost, I discovered the power of neuroplasticity and how it could help individual to take advantage of opportunities to stimulate the brain to change to improve cognitive functions, mental health, and memory, ultimately leading to a better and more productive life (Psychology Today Staff, 2022).

I praise You;
for I am fearfully and wonderfully made; Marvelous are Your works,
And that my soul knows very well.
Psalm 139:14

CHAPTER 12

The Brain

Research has firmly established that the brain is a highly adaptable organ and can reshape itself in response to experiences through a process called neuroplasticity, also referred to as brain plasticity, or neural plasticity. This remarkable process is the brain's ability to modify its structure, function, and organization considering the various experiences encountered throughout the individual's lifespan. This allows the brain to adapt to new situations and learning can occur at different stages of development from infancy to adulthood.

I discovered the power of neuroplasticity and began to employ techniques to improve my own life and made promises to myself to challenge my brain with new, stimulating and fulfilling activities particularly in retirement years. This is an important aspect of generativity in senior years to combat feelings of loneliness or isolation and reduce cognitive decline that can be common in the older age.

Some suggested activities are as follows:

1. Engage in lifelong learning: I revisited passions that had lay dormant to form new connections in my brain. I began learning new skills and techniques of playing the piano. I switched from being a classically trained pianist to learning techniques for different styles of music. I've enjoyed reading, sewing, crafts, and gardening, so I'm in search of a quilting guild and will start projects of quilt making. I'm looking forward to reading, sharing knowledge and skills to connect and stimulate the neurons, so I am hoping to reconnect with the Women of Wisdom or hoping to start a local book club.

2. Exercise Regularly: Science continues to show that physical exercise has been shown to have positive effects on brain health and neuroplasticity by increasing the blood flow to the brain, releasing, and enhancing the formation of new neurons and neural connections. So, I've joined the Montclair Walkers and walk 1 hour three days a week in the mall moving from that comfortable sedentary life

3. Maintain Healthy Diet: Nutrients, supplements, antioxidants and omega-3 fatty acids support brain health and neuroplasticity. Foods like fruits, vegetable, whole grains, eat proteins and healthy fats provide nutrients for optimal brain function. It is also important to avoid alcohol, drugs, and over-prescribed legal medications and excessive dopamine stimulation to not disrupt the brain's natural reward system.

4. Meditation Promotes Neuroplasticity. Reading daily devotions and applying the word of God to situations and circumstances have proven to reduce stress, improve focus and enhance the overall brain functions.

5. Restful Sleep: Sleep is crucial for brain health and neuroplasticity. It is during sleep that the brain consolidates memories, repairs, and rejuvenates itself and removes toxins. So, it is important to have a sleep schedule to support brain functioning and neuroplasticity (*Neuroplasticity* by Cooper, N. (2019), Las Vegas, NV).

Finally, and foremost, while the impact of childhood trauma can have a profound effect on adults, healing and recovery are possible. There are many support networks and self-care practices that individuals can use to address and overcome the impacts of childhood trauma that can lead to a better quality of life.

CHAPTER 13

Reflection

Let's reflect upon the transformation process of the diamond, one of God's beautiful creations, also known as a gem or a rock. This jewel is one of the hardest substances on earth and is used in grinding and cutting. Some jewels find their way to earth from volcanic eruptions and people rush to mine for them all over the earth. Geologists believed that they started out as carbon deposited in underground pipes, compressed together enduring extreme temperatures and turned into a star. The diamond is a precious stone loved by man when discovered (Source: Nature and Science @www.KonnectHQ.com).

During life's journey, pressures come like a strong and mighty wind that can squeeze you or build you. These strong winds can come in the form of a heartbreak, illness, worry, unexpected loss, financial fall, or a broken relationship. It can tear the very core from your soul. Often people's response to these circumstances is to believe the lie and build a wall, which becomes a fortress or a stronghold, become fearful and operate in denial that only God can remove.

The goal of the Believer is to become like that diamond and be transformed into the image and likeness of Christ. When we accept Jesus Christ as our Lord and Savior and receive the gift of the Holy Spirit, we are transformed and have a divine identity because we are now a born-again child of the Most High God. We must learn to come into a personal relationship with Him. We no longer depend on our knowledge of Him, but we are to grow in our consciousness of the Holy Spirit. For it is in Him that we now live and move and have our being.

Jesus calls the Holy Spirit the Spirit of Truth. The Holy Spirit comes to us on three different levels. He is *with* us (convicts of sin), He is *in* us (new birth) and He is *upon* us (in fullness). His function is to lead and guide us into all truth. Additionally, He is called the Spirit of Wisdom, the Spirit of Understanding, the Spirit of Knowledge, and the Spirit of Judgment. We are now seated in heavenly places. We live, move, and His being operates through us in the earth realm. We all have a divine purpose, and we need to operate in the power of the Holy Spirit to carry out the will of our heavenly Father through our Lord, here on earth. We are ambassadors of Christ. Our citizenship is the kingdom of God. We have been called out of the world system into the kingdom of God.

Our purpose is to thirst for God's way and do what is right as we take dominion. We must renew our minds and change any negative mindset that has kept us from walking in divine authority and power. God has given and empowered us with divine gifts, talents, and abilities, which enables us to let our lights so shine before men, women, boys, and girls, so they can not only see but do the good and greater works and glorify our Father God in heaven. We have power and influence over the atmosphere and the environments we occupy.

Deliverance from under the *Lingering Shadow* opened the door to the unlimited divine power we have through the Holy Spirit, which causes us to live from the inside out. We have the Mind of Christ, His Wisdom and His Nature and Character, which enables us to do and be all we can think or imagine. We can move from glory to glory becoming more and more like His image. The Kingdom of God operates through us, we have that same power and authority over that lingering shadow, over the power of the enemy, the flesh and principalities, powers and the rulers of the darkness of this world system that operate in the earth realm.

God created man in His own Image and in His Likeness.
Genesis 1:26, 27 (NKJV)

For we do not wrestle against flesh and blood, but against principalities,
against powers, against the rulers of the darkness of this age,
against spiritual hosts of wickedness in the heavenly places.
Ephesians 6:12 NKJV

CHAPTER 14

The Clarion Call To Kingdom Living

I have called you to go forth.

My heart has healed, and my spirit reinvigorated, allowing me finally to answer the clarion call resonating within me. In times past, the clarion call was the blowing of a trumpet to summon followers to a holy assembly, to warn them of impending danger or to announce that the king is arriving. It's time to move from complacency. Stop procrastinating. Stop being fearful. Stop imposing limitations on ourselves. Neglecting God's calling is no longer an option.

Has life hardened your heart to the extent that you can no longer sense His presence or respond to His touch? Listen closely, for we all have the responsibility to demolish the fortifications we've built around our hearts. Knowledge is powerful. All of us have been fearfully and wonderfully made with a brain that can change and grow in response to life experiences. You were created to bounce back from setbacks and adversity. The time has come to move away from the kingdom of this world system and into the Kingdom of

God that rules and reigns from the inside out. It's time to rise up and conquer.

Jesus is seeking a new generation to embrace the mantel of leadership as Kings and Priests. Can He count on you?

CHAPTER 15

The Prayer

Father, in the Name of Jesus, I thank You and praise You and give You all the glory and honor You so richly deserve. I thank You, Father God, that I have yielded myself to You to be a vessel to be used as I tell my story and to show how Your hand has moved in my life since I was a child, and you have been changing me to conform into Your Image and likeness. I thank You for all the people that have come into my life to help and encourage me to stay the course. I thank You for the precious Holy Spirit that has led me, guided me, instructed me, convicted me, comforted me, and now, healed my heart, making it pliable and I have experienced a change for Your purpose.

I pray that the goal of this book was met, and many will see the impact of childhood trauma. Most importantly, people will see the mindset: The *Lingering Shadow* of the dysfunctional patterns of thinking and behavior that seemingly had been difficult to change. The lingering shadow has been like a river where the water flows, but back up because there are tree limbs, dirt and rocks which represents trial and challenges in life. Disappointments are symbolic of the broken limbs, rocks, dirt; and all the stuff that prevents the water from flowing naturally. As a result, the water will stop flowing and become stagnant. Utilizing the power of neuroplasticity is like finding a new channel for the water to flow again by restructuring, revamping, and moving to a new part of the brain. The power of neuroplasticity allows the brain to rewire and continue to form new neural connections and pathways for new learning, growing, adapting and recovery from the impact of trauma and challenges. Recovery can lead to developing a new mindset with improved motor skills, increase creativity, language, enhance memories and cognitive functions that can lead to a better quality of life.

Finally, and foremost, we need to feed our spirit man by meditating on and applying the principles of the word of God to experience a transformation in our thinking, actions and attitudes.

But seek ye first the Kingdom of God, and his righteousness;
and all these things will be added to you.
Matthew 6:33 NKJV 1

I beseech you therefore, brethren, by the mercies of God, that you present
your bodies a living sacrifice, holy, acceptable to God, which is your
reasonable service. 2) And do not be conformed to this world,
but be transformed by the renewing of your mind, that you may prove
what is that good and acceptable and perfect will of God.
Romans 12:1-2 NKJV

CHAPTER 16

The Results

Meditation can also bring about changes. Speaking scriptures is one solution to beginning the healing process when dealing with cognitive distortions, irrational thought patterns or core beliefs. We can do as James 1:58 says, "*If any of you lack wisdom, let him ask of God, that giveth to all men liberally, and without reproach, and it will be given to him. But let him ask in faith, without doubting, for he who doubts is like a wave of the sea driven and tossed by the wind. For let not that man suppose that he will receive anything from the Lord; He is a doubleminded man, unstable in all his ways.*"

Emotions, distorted thoughts, and behaviors can tempt us to take the easy way, to do what feels good for the moment. Wisdom moves us to take the way that seems hard at first, but later we find that it leads to life. Seek Scriptures to confess daily to change the negative thoughts and subsequently, the behaviors.

But the wisdom that comes from heaven is first of all pure; then peace-loving, considerate, submissive, full of mercy and good fruit, impartial and sincere.
James 3:17 (NIV)

CHAPTER 17

The Devotions

My child, come, sit, and sup with me. 'Imagine that you have been given a beautiful, expensive robe that covers you completely. The cost of this robe was the sacrifice Jesus made on the cross. It cannot be earned through good works, for it is His gift to you. Sometimes, you might feel uncomfortable in the robe and forget that you have been given such a great honor. Instead of trying to get rid of the robe, remember to focus on Jesus and let the comfort of the robe remind you of your position in His kingdom. If you do something that isn't fitting for someone in His kingdom, don't take off the robe but throw off the unrighteous way of thinking, change your attitude, and foremost, change your behavior so that it will match your position.' (Young, 2016).

Do not conform any longer to the pattern of this world,
but be transformed by the renewing of your mind. Then you will be able
to test and approve what God's will is—
His good, pleasing, and perfect will.
Romans 12:2 (NIV)

COMMON COGNITIVE DISTORTIONS

Devotions and Challenge Exercises:

1. Use the **Common Cognitive Distortions (Appendix 1)** to identify thoughts, patterns, and behaviors that are contrary to God's way of thinking and acting.

2. Carefully and prayerfully, consider the list and identify any area where you repeatedly experience difficulty.

3. What is God saying to you about thoughts and behaviors that need changing?

4. Consider what Scriptures you can apply to areas of your life that have been resistant to change.

Prayer of Confession: Find Scriptures to pray and confess to change cognitive distortions.

EVALUATING CORE BELIEFS

Devotion and Challenge Exercises:

1. Use the **Evaluation of Core Beliefs (Appendix 2)** to identify thoughts, patterns, and behaviors that are contrary to God's way of thinking and acting.

2. Carefully and prayerfully, identify any area where you repeatedly experience difficulty.

3. What is God saying to you about thoughts and behaviors that need changing?

4. Consider what Scriptures you can apply to areas of your life that have been resistant to change.

Prayer of Confession: Find Scriptures to pray and confess daily until you receive the manifestation of the changed thoughts or behaviors.

FAULTY CORE BELIEFS ASSESSMENT

Devotion and Challenge Exercises:
Use **Faulty Core Beliefs Assessment** to identify thoughts, patterns, and behaviors that are contrary to God's way of thinking and acting.

1. Carefully and prayerfully identify any area where you repeatedly experience difficulty.

2. What is God saying to you about thoughts and behaviors that need changing?

3. Consider what Scriptures you can apply to areas of your life that have been resistant to change.

Prayer of Confession: Find Scriptures to pray and confess daily.

APPENDIX 1

COMMON COGNITIVE DISTORTIONS THAT CAN CAUSE NEGATIVE THINKING FROM SCIENTIFIC PERSPECTIVE.

Assessment of 10 Common Cognitive Distortions

MENTAL FILTERING is when someone focuses only on the negative parts of a conversation or situation and ignores the positive aspects. This type of negative thinking can develop over time and become a response to difficult circumstances. It can cause a person to have an overly dark and pessimistic view of the world.

POLARIZATION occurs when individuals or groups develop extreme, opposing, or divisive viewpoints that are in direct conflict with each other. This can lead to a lack of cooperation, communication and understanding between people or groups with differing opinions, ultimately leading to division and conflict. It can also make it difficult for individuals to accept or understand anyone who holds opposing views, causing further tension and conflict.

DISCOUNTING THE POSITIVE is where someone downplays, discredits, or dismisses their own accomplishments or positive attributes, despite external evidence or feedback from others. They may perceive a situation as negative and the good and positive aspects are rejected because they insist that the good doesn't count. This distorted pattern of thinking disregards the success and focuses on weaknesses and failures. It is important to recognize the challenges in the areas that could have been done better, completely ignoring their success.

JUMPING TO CONCLUSIONS is interpreting things negatively when there are no facts to support your conclusion. This is a common issue that many people have. People make premature assumptions that are unwarranted because their viewpoint is based on limited information. They jump to a conclusion because they do not have all the facts and assume things that are not true.

CATASTROPHIZING is a thought pattern where a person believes that a situation is much worse than it is, and that the worst possible outcome is inevitable. Catastrophizing often involves excessive worry and anxiety and can lead to feelings of being overwhelmed, hopelessness and helplessness. It can also lead to negative behaviors such as avoidance and procrastination.

PERSONALIZATION is the belief that occurs when you hold yourself personally responsible for an event that isn't entirely under your control. It can be interpreting a remark or action that was directed against oneself and becoming upset or offended by it. Situation or circumstances can occur, and a person can think it is about them when it isn't.

BLAMING is another cognitive distortion, faulty thought pattern or behavior that causes a person to wrongly assign the responsibility of a negative outcome either to oneself or another. This cognitive distortion occurs when one wrongly blames another for one's own actions. The individual deflects his own responsibility onto another.

It can also mean to find fault with; to censure or to criticize; to make a claim of wrongdoing or misbehavior against. Some individuals want to be the victim. We see that the victim blames what other people do when they cannot accept responsibility or the consequences of their own action.

EMOTIONAL REASONING is a conclusion that the emotional reaction of an individual proves something is true, despite the evidence showing that it is false. Emotional reasoning is irrational as it focuses on the emotions involved and not on common sense. Often, emotional reasoning can be the trigger that can cause one to get angry at the drop of a hat, resulting in unforgiveness in that person's heart.

ALWAYS BEING RIGHT is another irrational way of thinking and is characterized by the need to always prove oneself right to prove others' opinions are wrong. People with this unrealistic mindset cannot accept that they can make mistakes. Hence, they will do everything in their power to prove that others are wrong. This behavior can cause people to turn against you.

LABELING refers to the act of passing judgment on a person's character or their personality instead of viewing their behavior as a separate entity for the opinion or fact does not define them wholly. Making the judgment about the individual because of behavior does not define the person wholly. Labeling is a confirmation bias that overlooks contradictory evidence and focuses solely on negative thoughts. It is essential to differentiate between opinions and facts. An example is when you might label yourself as a failure you label other people as a failure as well, instead of looking for evidence that counters your negative thoughts. There are opinions and there are facts.

It is essential to differentiate between opinions and facts.

Hartney, E. (2022)

APPENDIX 2

Evaluation of Core Beliefs

Core beliefs are a person's most central ideas about themselves, others, and the world. These beliefs act like a lens through which every situation and life experience is seen. Because of this, people with different core beliefs might be in the same situation, but think, feel, and behave very differently. Even if a core belief is accurate, it still shapes how a person sees the world. Harmful core beliefs lead to negative thoughts, feelings, and behaviors, whereas rational core beliefs lead to balanced reactions.

Situation: Two people with different core beliefs receive a bad grade on a test.

Person	Core Belief	Reaction
A	"I am a failure."	**Thought**: *Of course, I failed ...why bother?* **Feeling:** Depression **Behavior:** Makes no change.
B	I am perfectly capable when "I give my best effort."	**Thought**: *I did poorly because I didn't prepare.* **Feeling:** Disappointment **Behavior:** Plans to study before the next test.

Common Harmful Core Beliefs

Core beliefs are often hidden beneath surface-level beliefs. For example, the core belief "no one likes me" might underlie the surface belief "my friends only spend time with me out of pity".

Helpless
"I am weak"
"I am a loser"

Unlovable
"I am unlovable"
"I will end up alone"

Worthless
"I am bad"
"I don't deserve to live"

External Danger
"The world is dangerous"
"People can't be trusted"

Consequences of Harmful Core Beliefs

Interpersonal Problems:

- Difficulty trusting others
- Feelings of inadequacy in relationships
- Excessive jealousy
- Overly confrontational or aggressive
- Putting others' needs about one's own needs

Mental Health Problems:

- Depression
- Substance Abuse
- Anxiety
- Difficulty handling stress
- Low self-esteem

Facts About Core Beliefs

- People are not born with core beliefs – they are learned.
- Core beliefs usually develop in childhood, or during stressful or traumatic periods in adulthood.
- Information that contradicts core beliefs is often ignored.
- Negative core beliefs are not necessarily true, even if they feel true.
- Core beliefs tend to be rigid and long-standing. However, they can be changed.

APPENDIX 3

FAULTY CORE BELIEFS ASSESSMENT

This exercise is designed to help you identify areas where a faulty core belief or erroneous mindset may be occurring. These beliefs or mindsets should be examined to eliminate any hindrances to growth or changes you may wish to make in those areas. Carefully and prayerfully, consider the list below and check each area where you **repeatedly** experience difficulty:

___ Relationship with the Godhead

___ Fellowshipping with Jesus Christ

___ Family Relationships

___ Committed Relationships

___ Work relationships

___ Monetary Issues

___ Self-Esteem/Self Valuing Issues

___ Indecisiveness

___ Fear

___ Parent/Child Issues

___ Physical Image

___ Physical Health

___ Lack of Direction or Focus

___ Friendships

___ Personal Security

___ Unhappiness/Depression

___ Forgiveness

___ Self-confidence

___ Thoughts, confusion

___ Feelings

___ Undisciplined Behavior

___ Sleep, Food

References

American Counseling Association. (2014). *ACA code of ethics.* https://www.counseling.org/resources/aca-code-of-ethics.pdf

American Legal (2202). *Abandonment of Refrigerators and Iceboxes in Places Accessible to Children* https://codelibrary.amlegal.com

American Psychiatric Association (APA) (2022). *Diagnostic and Statistical Manual of Mental Disorders: Dsm-5-Tr.* Published: Washington, DC

Anda (2022). *The "Crucifixion" – The Largest Painting Ever Painted.* Published by Travel Notes Beyond. Retrieved from Website: https://www.travelnotesandbeyond.com

Centers for Disease Control and Prevention (CDC, 2019). National Center for Prevention and Control. *Adverse Childhood Experiences (ACEs) Preventing Early Trauma to Improve Adult Health.* Vitalsigns

Chand, et al., (2022). *Cognitive Behavior Therapy.* National Library of Medicine. Retrieved from: www.ncbi.nlm.nih.gov

Coalition for National Trauma Research (CNTR, 2022), San Antonio, TX. (Rep.) *Trauma Statistics & Facts.*

Cook, et al., (2005). *Complex Trauma in Children and Adolescents* – APA PsycNet. Retrieved from www.doi.org/10.3928/00485713-20050501-05

Cooper, N., (2023) In italics, Neuroplasticity, Las Vegas, NV.

Dugal, C., Bigras, N., Godbout, N., & Bélanger, C. (2016). *Childhood Interpersonal Trauma and its Repercussions in Adulthood: An Analysis of Psychological and Interpersonal Sequelae. A multidimensional approach to post-traumatic stress disorder – from theory to practice.* Retrieved from: https://doi.org/10.5772/64476

Gillette, G. (2021). *What is EMDR Therapy?* Published by: PsychCentral

Gonzalez-Prendes, A (2012). S*oc Work Values Ethics.* 9(2). Published by: Verywell

Hartney, E. (2022). *10 Cognitive Distortions That Can Cause Negative*

Thinking. Published by www.Verywellmind.com

International Society for Traumatic Stress Studies (ISTSS). *Traumatic Stress and Substance Abuse Problems,* Retrieved March 23, 2023, from www.istss.org/

ISTSS_Main/media/Documents/ISTSS_TraumaStressandSubstanceAbus eProb_English.NL

John Hopkins Medicine (2023). *Baby Blues and Postpartum Depression: Mood Disorders and Pregnancy.* Retrieved May 27, 2023,Women's

Health www.hopkinsmedicine.org/health/wellness-and-prevention

Jones, B. (2021). *Childhood Trauma: Signs You're Repressing Traumatic*

Memories. Published by and retrieved from www.verywellhealth.com

KonnectHQ.com. (Source*: Nature and Science* @www.KonnectHQ.com)

Lewis, M., Jones, R., Davis, M. (2020). *Exploring the Impact of Trauma Type and Extent of Exposure on Posttraumatic Alterations in 5-HT1A expression. Translational/Psychiatry* www.doi.org/10.1038/s41398-020-00915-1

Lifebuilders' Counseling Services, (2008). *Appendix 3: Core Beliefs Assessment*

Moore, K. (2021). *Declared Insane for Speaking Up: The Dark American History of Silencing Women Through Psychiatry.* Retrieved from website: www.time.com

Morin, A. (2022). *Treating the Effects of Childhood Trauma.* Website: www.verywell.com

McLean, C. & Foa, E. (2022). *Prolonged Exposure Therapy for PostTraumatic Stress Disorder: A Review of Evidence and Dissemination.* Expert Review of Neurotherapeutics, 11(8), 1151-1163. Retrieved from website: www.PsychologyToday.com

National Alliance for the Mentally Ill (NAMI), United States,

National Guidelines for Behavioral Health Crisis Care Best Practice Toolkit. (2020). SAMHSA-Substance Abuse and Mental Health Services Administration https://www.samhsa.gov/sites/default/files/national-guidelines-forbehavioral-health-crisis-care-02242020.pdf

Nelson, J. (1974). *Nixon Resigns in "interesis of nations."* LA Times (1923-Current File) August 9, 1974; ProQuest Historical Newspaper Los Angeles Times (1881-1987) Pg A1

Osborne, L. (2023). *Baby Blues and Postpartum Depression: Mood Disorders and Pregnancy.* https://www.hopkinsmedicine.org.

Otgaar, H., Howe, M., Patihis, L., et al. (2019). *The Return of the Repressed: The Persistent and Problematic Claims of Long-forgotten Trauma.* Perspectives on Psychological Science. 2019; 14(6):1072-1095. doi:10.1177/1745691619862306

Peterson, S. (2018, June 11). Effects. The National Child Traumatic Stress Network. from https://www.nctsn.org/what-is-child-trauma/traumatypes/complex-trauma/effects

Psychology Today Staff (2023). *Neuroplasticity.* Sussex Publishers, LLC Ritter., R. M. (2014). *New Oxford Dictionary for Writers and editors.* Oxford University Press. Scriptures marked (NKJV) are taken from the New King James Version – Copyright ©1982 by Thomas Nelson. Used by Permission. All rights reserved.

Simone, M. (2021). *What Are the Best Types of Therapy for Trauma?* Retrieved from: www.psychcentral.com

Substance Abuse and Mental Health Services Administration (SAMHSA, 2014), U.S. Department of Retrieved website: https://www.samhsa.gov/child-trauma/understanding-child-trauma-Substance Abuse and Mental Health Services Administration (SAMHSA), (2022). *Traumatic Stress and Substance Abuse Problems.* Retrieved from website: www.samhsa.gov/resource/dbhis/traumatic-stress-substanceabuse-problems

Therapist Aid (2020). ***Appendix 2:*** *What are Core Beliefs?*

Therapist Aid, (2021). Retrieved from website: www.Therapistaid.com

Vitelli, R. (2012). *How Can We Treat Traumatized Children? Treating Children for Traumatic Experiences Can Prevent Later Problems.*

Young, S. (2015). *Jesus Calling: Enjoying Peace in His Presence.*

Publisher: Thomas Nelson

Zemeckis, R. (1994). *Tom Hank as Forrest Gump*. Paramount Pictures

To the Reader:

I pray my memoir will inspire you, as well as enlighten your awareness of things unseen but most importantly, broaden and deepen your faith in God and His Son, Jesus Christ. I pray that your desire to trust Christ through all aspects of your life has been strengthened and solidified.

Just know that God truly is faithful. He will give you victory if you will only stand and be immovable in Him. Stand in the midst of your trials suited in the armor of God, well fitted and knowing that you are more than a conqueror. You can do all things through Christ who strengthens you. To God be the Glory!

About the Author:

My career and professional achievements have been working a combined 34 years with the County of Los Angeles with Clerk's Office and County Counsel's Office for 17 years and later with the City of Los Angeles as an Administrative Support person with Department of Contract Compliance and the Board of Public Works. Two years between the two employments were spent working as a Secretary with Rockwell International for the Space Program.

In response to the call of God, I earned a master's in biblical studies and a Doctor of Ministry in Professional Faith-Based Biblical Counseling with an emphasis in Pastoral Counseling from Friends International Christian University. I am certified by the Board of Behavioral Sciences through LifeBuilders' Counseling Institute by Marriage-Family Therapist, the late Dr. Doris Morgan, Ph.D., as a Professional Faith-Based Biblical Counselor. I volunteered as a Professional Biblical Counselor at the Betty R. Price Counseling Center under the supervision of the late Dr. Doris Morgan. I returned to Grand Canyon University and earned a master's degree in Addiction and worked as a Drug and Alcohol Counselor at Behavioral Health Services.

In addition, I taught Bible study to children for over thirty years and was instrumental in getting the first afterschool Bible club into the public-school system in Lancaster, California with over 100 children attending weekly. I have also worked as a volunteer with Chaplain Emertha Jones at Challenger Memorial Youth Prison Center in Lancaster, CA with the troubled and incarcerated youth from the ages of 13–17.

After years of service, I was motivated to answer the call to minister to bruised and broken individuals. I earned a master's degree in Addiction Counseling and a Bachelor of Science in Chemical Dependency and Substance Abuse with an emphasis in Addiction from Grand Canyon University. In addition, I became certified by the State of California through California Consortium of Addiction Programs and Professionals (CCAPP) and worked at the Behavioral Health Services-South Bay Recovery Center as an Alcohol and Drug Counselor/Addiction Specialist until my retirement in June 2022.

9 798822 942196

Printed by Libri Plureos GmbH in Hamburg, Germany